Sakura Taisen Manga Version Volume One
Table of Contents

Vol. 1

Story by
Ohji Hiroi

Art by
Ikku Masa

Characters by
Kosuke Fujishima

HAMBURG // LONDON // LOS ANGELES // TOKYO

Sakura Taisen Vol. 1
Story by Ohji Hiroi
Art by Ikku Masa
Characters by Kosuke Fujishima

Translation - Yuko Fukami
Retouch and Lettering - Irene Woori Choi
Production Artist - James Lee
Cover Design - Jorge Negrete

Editor - Lillian Diaz-Przybyl
Digital Imaging Manager - Chris Buford
Pre-Press Manager - Antonio DePietro
Production Managers - Jennifer Miller and Mutsumi Miyazaki
Art Director - Matt Alford
Managing Editor - Jill Freshney
VP of Production - Ron Klamert
Editor-in-Chief - Mike Kiley
President and C.O.O. - John Parker
Publisher and C.E.O. - Stuart Levy

A Manga

TOKYOPOP Inc.
5900 Wilshire Blvd. Suite 2000
Los Angeles, CA 90036

E-mail: info@TOKYOPOP.com
Come visit us online at www.TOKYOPOP.com

ISBN: 1-59816-484-8

First TOKYOPOP printing: December 2005
10 9 8 7 6 5 4 3 2 1
Printed in the USA

7

8

pachik

DIS-
TANCE,
300.

NUMBER
OF
ENEMIES,
TEN...
MAYBE?

THIS IS
WHEN
YOU FEEL
TRULY
ALIVE!

THE
TENSION
OF
COMBAT...

MAN,
THIS IS
THE LIFE,
OGAMI!

AFFIR-
MATIVE.

13

WHOOPS! TOO CLOSE.

LET'S GET 'EM BACK FOR THAT POTSHOT.

HEH HEH...

ON THE BATTLEFIELD, VICTORY IS FOR THE SIDE THAT MAKES AN ACCURATE ANALYSIS OF THE SITUATION.

THEY DON'T KNOW OUR POSITION YET.

NO.

DON'T RETURN FIRE YET.

C'MON, ARE YOU KIDDING?

SOME BLAZE OF GLORY. DO YOU WANT ALL OF US TO GO DOWN WITHOUT GETTING OFF A SINGLE ROUND?

HUH?!

WE SHOULD SNEAK AROUND BEHIND AND...

THEY'VE GOT A STEAM TANK?!

WHAT THE...

15

EED!

URK!

THERE ARE NO RULES IN REAL WAR.

BLAST! THOSE OFFICERS ARE PLAYING DIRTY!

NO WAY WE CAN BEAT A WEAPON LIKE THAT!

THERE ARE ALWAYS UNKNOWN FACTORS IN A COMBAT ZONE.

ISN'T USING STEAM TANKS AGAINST THE RULES?

THE DRILL-MASTERS ARE JUST SCREWING AROUND WITH US!

C'MON OGAMI, THIS IS A TOTAL FARCE.

A SOLDIER MUST ALWAYS CARRY OUT HIS MISSION, NO MATTER WHAT!

BESIDES, OUR MISSION IS TO DESTROY THE ENEMY.

18

19

NOW POUND THAT STEAM TANK, KAYAMA!!

PERFECT!

INCOMING!

22

EVEN A TANK'S PRETTY USELESS...

...IF YOU CAN'T SEE OUT OF IT!

YOU'RE DEAD MEAT.

GET UP, KAYAMA.

BAH...

--TCH ...

OOH HUH HUH HUH...

26

Headquarters

THIS CONCLUDES THE NAVAL ACADEMY'S SPECIAL NIGHTTIME BATTLE SIMULATION.

ALL STUDENTS ARE ORDERED TO RETURN TO THE MAIN UNIT, BATHE AND PREPARE FOR THE GRADUATION PARTY!

GOT IT? I *DIDN'T* LOSE!

YOU RAN OUT OF TIME! YOU DIDN'T BEAT ME!!

Hurrah!

......

HUMPH!

27

Edajima

Naval
Academy

29

NO...

IT'S BEEN PERFECTLY CHILLED.

I'LL PASS THIS TIME.

YOU WANT SOME, OGAMI?

YUP.

SO WE'RE FINALLY GRADUATING.

HA HA HA

WA HA HA HA HA

HAVE YOU SUBMITTED A POSTING REQUEST, KAYAMA?

HA HA HA HA!

· · · · ·

BWAH HA HA HA!

HEH HEH HEH...

PFFT!

"THE FUTURE IS UNKNOWN," EH?

· · · · ·

...IT AIN'T GONNA BE EASY. BETTER WORK HARD, OGAMI.

EVEN AFTER WE GRADU- ATE...

YEP.

35

SIGNED, MINISTER OF THE NAVY, KAZUTOYO YAMAGUCHI.

THE AFORE-MENTIONED PERSONNEL IS TO SERVE AT THE GRAND IMPERIAL THEATRE.

ICHIRO OGAMI!

YOU MEAN *THE* LIEUTENANT GENERAL YONEDA, THE LEGENDARY LIONHEART?

YONEDA...

WE'RE COUNTING ON YOU TO DO YOUR VERY BEST.

FROM THIS DAY ON, YOU WILL BE UNDER THE COMMAND OF LIEUTENANT GENERAL IKKI YONEDA.

THE GRAND IMPERIAL THEATRE? WHAT DOES THAT--

B-BUT...

THIS IS A *SPECIAL* ASSIGNMENT.

NO QUESTIONS, AND DEFINITELY NO REFUSALS ARE PERMITTED.

!!

I, ICHIRO OGAMI, SHALL DO MY UTMOST TO SERVE MY POST, SIRS!

UNDER-STOOD, SIR!

SOMEONE FROM LIEUTENANT GENERAL YONEDA'S STAFF WILL CONTACT YOU.

WAIT FOR WORD IN FRONT OF THE STATUE OF SAIGO* AT UENO PARK IN FOUR DAYS.

*A FAMOUS SAMURAI WARRIOR FROM THE END OF THE MEIJI ERA.

Tokyo,
The
Imperial
Capital

40

IS THIS GIRL PART OF LIEUTENANT GENERAL YONEDA'S STAFF?

A CIVILIAN....?

SORRY, I MUST HAVE MADE A MISTAKE.

OH. AH HA HA HA...

. . . . .

. . . . .

WELL, I...

I AM ICHIRO OGAMI.

WHO ARE YOU?

WHERE COULD HE BE?

I FORGOT THE PHOTO, SO I CAN'T TELL BY HIS FACE...

WHAT AM I GOING TO DO?

ACTUALLY, NO...

42

YOU'RE KIND OF STARING...

DO I HAVE SOMETHING ON MY FACE?

UM... UMM

OGAMI-SAN?

HUH?

ERR... NO, UM...

I MEAN...

WHA--?

WHOA!

OH, YOU SILLY! DON'T TEASE ME LIKE THAT!

I REALLY LUCKED OUT WITH THIS NEW POSTING.

THE...

SAKURA'RE AWFULLY PRETTY AROUND HERE!

HEY...

WAIT FOR ME!

BUT WE'RE RIGHT IN THE MIDDLE OF THE GINZA!

WHAT, HERE...?

THIS IS IT!

WELCOME TO THE GRAND IMPERIAL THEATER!

A LAND-MARK...

OF COURSE. THE IMPERIAL IS ONE OF GINZA'S MOST FAMOUS LAND-MARKS.

I THOUGHT THAT THE GRAND IMPERIAL THEATER WAS SOME KIND OF CODE NAME, BUT...

IT'S REALLY JUST A THEATER!

The Grand Imperial Opera Troupe Hanagumi Presentation April 1923

The Twilight of Princess Tsubaki

Starring Sumire Kanzaki (Margritte)

(A revival production)

BUT...!

I DON'T GET IT.

COULD THIS REALLY BE A MILITARY BASE?

IN SUCH A PROMINENT LOCATION, TOO...

ONCE WE GO INSIDE, YOU CAN SEE HER IN PERSON.

OGAMI-SAN, YOU NEEDN'T STARE SO HARD AT SUMIRE-SAN'S PICTURE.

WHAT ON EARTH IS LIEUTENANT GENERAL YONEDA UP TO HERE? WHAT SORT OF SPECIAL ASSIGNMENT IS THIS?!

WHY WAS I ASSIGNED TO A **THEATER**, OF ALL PLACES?

AND WHERE IS LIEUTENANT GENERAL YONEDA?

I SEE.

IT MAY BE EMPTY NOW, BUT RIGHT BEFORE A PERFORMANCE, IT'S SO FULL OF PATRONS THAT YOU CAN BARELY GET THROUGH THE CROWD.

IM-PRES-SIVE, ISN'T IT?

WOW, WHAT A HUGE LOBBY!

M-MAN-AGER?

THAT'S THE RULE!

AROUND HERE, YOU HAVE TO CALL HIM "MANAGER."

OGAMI-SAN, I MUST TELL YOU SOME-THING...

PLEASE GO AHEAD TO THE MANAGER'S OFFICE. IT'S RIGHT NEXT TO THE CAFETERIA.

IF YOU'LL PARDON ME...

GOOD, YOU'RE BACK.

OH, SAKURA-SAN!

OH, OKAY!

WE NEED YOU FOR A WIG FITTING.

I BET IT'S INTELLIGENCE WORK.

THIS THEATER MUST BE JUST A FRONT FOR THE ACTIVITIES.

SO IT'S "MANAGER YONEDA," THEN, EH? I THINK I GET IT.

WHO WAS OFFENDED?

INTELLIGENCE... AFFRONT?

52

HOW CAN SHE KNOW ABOUT ME?!

WH—WHAT IS THIS GIRL?

HOW CAN I INDEED!

TEE HEE HEE!

......

GULP!

SHOULD I TELL YOU?

DO YOU WANT TO KNOW HOW I KNOW ABOUT YOU?

53

54

THE MANAGER HAS BEEN WAITING FOR YOU.

YOU MUST BE ENSIGN OGAMI.

SLAM

AND YOU ARE...?

IT'S A PLEASURE.

MY NAME IS MARIA TACHIBANA.

SHE KIND OF LOOKED LIKE SHE HAD SOMETHING AGAINST ME. SUCH COLD EYES...

A FOREIGNER...?

I WONDER IF SHE'S PART OF THE MISSION?

I MUST SEE LIEUTENANT GENERAL YONEDA AND HAVE HIM EXPLAIN EVERYTHING.

SHOOT! THAT STRANGE KID AND THIS WOMAN... EVERYTHING'S TOTALLY OVER MY HEAD TODAY!

IF THIS KEEPS UP, I'M GOING TO GO NUTS.

YOU OVER THERE!

YOU, BOY!

56

I DROPPED MY FORK!

PICK IT UP!

WHY ARE YOU JUST STANDING THERE?

glare

UH... YES'M?

EVEN WITH SUCH A SPLENDID BUILDING, THE THEATER IS NOTHING IF THE PEOPLE WORKING ON THE INSIDE ARE ALL FOOLS.

IT'S SUCH AN EMBARRASSMENT!!

UGH! THIS ESTABLISHMENT'S NEW EMPLOYEE TRAINING PROGRAM IS OBVIOUSLY GOING TO THE DOGS!

NOW, BRING ME A CLEAN ONE IMMEDIATELY!

58

OH, IT'S THAT ACTRESS...

COULD THIS DAME BE MORE RUDE?

SUMIRE SOMETHING-OR-OTHER WHO WAS ON THE BILLBOARD OUTSIDE.

AS OF TODAY, I AM TAKING UP A NEW POST HERE.

FORGIVE ME, BUT I AM NOT A WAITER!

ENSIGN ICHIRO OGAMI, REPORTING!

GOODNESS, PLEASE FORGIVE ME!

OH DEAR, I THOUGHT YOU WERE A NEW WAITER.

OH HO HO HO HO!

IT'S ALREADY TIME FOR THE DRESS REHEARSAL.

MY, MY!

IT'S OGAMI...

SINCE TODAY IS THE FIRST DAY OF THE REVIVAL SHOW, I'M RATHER PREOCCUPIED AT THE MOMENT...

I'M SO TERRIBLY SORRY, ENSIGN OGAWA!

GOOD DAY...

......

...'TSUMIRE' KANZAKI-SAN.

GOOD DAY, ENSIGN OGAWA!

BEGGING YOUR PARDON.

IT BE-HOOVES YOU TO REMEM-BER...

I AM AN ACTRESS!

THE TOP STAR OF THE IMPERIAL!

I DON'T IMAGINE THAT YOU WOULD LIKE IT IF SOMEONE MADE THE SAME MISTAKE WITH YOUR NAME, NOW WOULD YOU, ENSIGN OGAWA?!

MISTAKING THE NAME OF SUMIRE KANZAKI WILL SIMPLY NOT BE TOLERATED!!

MY NAME'S...

...OGAMI...

GOOD DAY!!

DO NOT MAKE SUCH A POOR JOKE OUT OF YOURSELF AGAIN.

ERGH...

Manager's Office

YES, SIR!!

YA REALLY WANNA KNOW?

I WOULD LIKE TO KNOW MORE ABOUT MY MISSION, PLEASE, SIR!!

YES, MY MISSION!!

HAH?

MIGHT AS WELL CHANGE INTO THIS FIRST.

I'M COUNTING ON YOU, OGAMI!

I PLAN TO HAVE YOU DO OTHER THINGS AROUND THE THEATER TOO, OF COURSE.

OUR PATRONS ARE GONNA BE HERE TO WATCH THE PERFORMANCE SOON.

YOUR MISSION IS TO COLLECT THEIR TICKETS ON THE WAY IN.

GOT IT? YOU'RE THE NEW TICKET TAKER.

66

I THINK YOU'RE A LITTLE CONFUSED, OGAMI.

INTELLIGENCE ACTIVITIES?

I MEAN, THE FACT THAT YOU'RE CALLING YOURSELF "MANAGER" MUST HAVE SOMETHING TO DO WITH THE SPECIAL MISSION...

SHOULD I THINK OF IT AS SOME KIND OF INTELLIGENCE ACTIVITY?

I GOT DISCHARGED A LONG TIME AGO. I'VE ONLY BEEN WORKING AS THE MANAGER OF THIS THEATER THANKS TO SOMEONE WHO OWED ME A FAVOR.

I'M JUST A PLAIN OL' WINO.

FIRST OFF, I'M NOT A LIEUTENANT GENERAL ANY MORE.

NO...

THAT CAN'T BE.

LOOKS LIKE WE GOT YOU, MR. HANDY-MAN.

...I ASKED MISUMI, WHO WAS MY SUBORDINATE IN THE ARMY, TO SEND ME SOMEONE YOUNG AND USEFUL WHO COULD HELP OUT WITH THE CHORES...

WE DON'T HAVE ENOUGH STRONG HANDS AT THE IMPERIAL, SO...

69

...AS A SUBORDINATE, IS IT YOUR PLACE TO CRITICIZE OR CORRECT IT?

EVEN WHEN A SUPERIOR OFFICER MAKES AN ERRONEOUS JUDGMENT...

IT'S A SOLDIER'S DUTY TO FOLLOW MILITARY REGULATIONS, ISN'T IT?

COME ON, OGAMI...

GLAD TO SEE YOU UNDER-STAND...

A SOLDIER MUST OBEY ORDERS AND BE LOYAL TO THE MISSION REGARDLESS!

A SOLDIER MUST...

I...

YOU'RE RIGHT, SIR.

YOU MAY NOT BE HAPPY ABOUT IT, BUT YOU HAVE TO OBEY ORDERS.

BUT THE DECISION HAS ALREADY BEEN MADE.

I FEEL BAD FOR YOU TOO.

YES, SIR.

I...

I, ENSIGN ICHIRO OGAMI...

SHALL HENCE-FORTH SERVE...

...AS THE TICKET TAKER AT THE GRAND IMPERIAL THEATER!!

HEY! WHAT'S GOING ON UP THERE?!

HOW LONG DOES IT TAKE TO CLIP A TICKET, YOU MORON?!

LET'S JUST PUSH OUR WAY THROUGH, BOSS!

CURSES! AT THIS RATE, WE'RE GOING TO MISS THE WHOLE SHOW! WE WON'T GET TO SEE MISS SUMIRE AS PRINCESS TSUBAKI!

GIVE ME A BREAK!

I CAN'T HELP IT IF I'VE NEVER DONE THIS BEFORE!

THIS IDIOT JUST ARRIVED FROM THE COUNTRY TODAY AND HE HASN'T LEARNED HIS MANNERS YET.

I AM THE HUMBLE MANAGER OF THIS THEATER.

FORGIVE ME! I AM SO TERRIBLY SORRY.

PLEASE FORGIVE HIM FOR MY SAKE, WON'T YOU, GENTLEMEN?

I AM VERY SORRY.

I...

YOU BETTER APOLOGIZE TO THE FINE SIRS!

OGAMI, YOU FOOL!!

IT'S NOT SOME CRUDE LOCAL OFFICE OR A MILITARY BASE!

THIS IS A FINE THEATER.

YOU SHOULD LEARN TO WATCH WHAT YOU SAY.

WELL, FARM-BOY!

76

WHY DO I HAVE TO BE HUMILIATED LIKE THIS?!

WHY?!

Ogami Arrives at the Imperial Capital—End of Act

Teikoku Kagekidan

大神 ＆ アイリス

Ogami
and
Iris

PHEW...

OH~~~

...SUCH A DREAMY...

...DECK~~~
...WASH~~~

DONE!

CHIRP

CHIRP

83

I'M REALLY, REALLY SORRY!

NO, NO...

IT'S FINE. YOU SHOULD REALLY GO CHANGE OUT OF THOSE WET THINGS, THOUGH.

AFTER ALL YOUR HARD WORK CLEANING, I GO AND MESS IT UP...

OH, I'M SORRY, OGAMI-SAN!

AW, MAN...

YOU THERE! ENSIGN OGATA!

ICHIRO OGAMI.

IT'S OGAMI...

ENSIGN OGATA!

DID YOU NOT HEAR ME?

SO, ENSIGN! I'M GOING TO THE MITSUKOSHI DEPARTMENT STORE THIS AFTERNOON. I WOULD LIKE YOU TO COME ALONG TO CARRY MY THINGS.

OH MY, IS THAT SO?

FINE. FROM NOW ON, I SHALL SIMPLY CALL YOU "ENSIGN" TO AVOID ANY CONFUSION, THEN!

86

HOW DARE YOU!!

I AM NOT YOUR SERVANT!

I DECLINE.

WHA--

I JUST HAVE A HARD TIME DEALING WITH HER.

S-SORRY.

YOU HAVE TO BE MORE POLITE TO SUMIRE-SAN! SHE'S THE STAR OF THE IMPERIAL!

COME ON, OGAMI-SAN!

OH HO HO HO!

OH MY!

ALL RIGHT...

WHEN SUMIRE-SAN GETS UPSET, WE ALL SUFFER, YOU KNOW!

GOOD MORNING!

AH! MANAGER!

YO, MY INDUSTRIOUS YOUNG MAN!

HOW'S LIFE TREATING YOU?

...STILL KIND OF UPTIGHT, AREN'T YOU?

THE CLEANING OF THE STAGE AND THE AUDITORIUM IS COMPLETE, SIR!

REALLY, SIR?!

RE--

IF I CAN MANAGE TO REMEMBER, I'LL SEE IF I CAN ARRANGE TO HAVE YOU GO BACK TO THE NAVY ONE OF THESE DAYS.

WELL, IT'S GOOD THAT YOU TAKE YOUR JOB SERIOUSLY, I SUPPOSE.

ガッカ

GOT-CHA!

89

AND SINCE THESE ARE HALF OF THE SAME-DAY TICKETS, THERE ARE 50 LEFT AND...

HALF OF SPECIAL SEATING IS 128 SEATS AND 14 OF THOSE ARE COMPLIMENTARY TICKETS...

SO...

WHAT DOES THIS MARK MEAN, KASUMI-KUN?

Office

THE FINAL TALLY FOR SAME-DAY SALES OF SPECIAL SEATING TICKETS IS 38 TICKETS.

...14 COMPLIMENTARY TICKETS MUST BE SUBTRACTED FROM THERE.

THAT MEANS, OF THE 128 SPECIAL SEATING, 52 ARE UNMARKED SAME-DAY TICKETS AND...

AND THIS IS THE CASH INCOME FOR FIRST TIER SEATS, AND THIS ONE FOR THE SECOND TIER SEATS.

SO, SINCE WE'VE RECEIVED MONEY ALREADY, THIS AMOUNT SHOULD BE TAKEN OFF YESTERDAY'S CASH INCOME AMOUNT.

THAT MEANS THOSE WERE BOUGHT IN ADVANCE.

AH, I GET IT.

90

OGAMI-SAN, YOU'RE THE KING OF ODD JOBS!!

WOW! FANTASTIC!

YOU MUST BE TIRED!

THANKS TO YOU, OGAMI-SAN, WE GOT THROUGH THE BOOKS MUCH FASTER THAN USUAL.

FIN-ISHED!

PHEW

I WANNA TELL HIM! I WANNA TELL HIM! I CAN'T STAND IT!

OH~~!!

NO THANKS. I'VE GOT OTHER CHORES TO TAKE CARE OF.

WELL, WOULD YOU CARE FOR A CUP OF TEA?

I'M NOT SURE HOW I FEEL ABOUT THAT, BUT...

KING OF ODD JOBS..

DON'T YOU THINK OGAMI-SAN WILL BE STUNNED WHEN HE FINDS OUT?

BUT KASUMI...

OOOH! I'M SO EXCITED!!

MANAGER YONEDA KNOWS WHAT HE'S DOING.

NO, YURI.

THAT'S A BAD HABIT OF YOURS.

YURI.

YES, MA'AM.

ONII-CHAN!

WON'T YOU STAY AND TALK TO ME?

BUT YOU CAN JUST CALL ME IRIS.

MY FULL NAME IS IRIS CHATEAU-BRIAND.

IRIS-CHAN, RIGHT?

OH, HEY!

HUH?

I'M NINE YEARS OLD.

HOW OLD ARE YOU, IRIS?

WELL...

I HAVE NO IDEA WHAT TO SAY TO SUCH A LITTLE GIRL.

WHAT SHOULD I DO?

· · · · · · ·

IS THAT SO?

THAT'S A REALLY CUTE RIBBON YOU HAVE ON!

HEY, IRIS.

UMMM... ERRR...

SHOOT! I GOTTA FIND AN OPENER...

BOOORING.

REALLY? YOU MEAN IT?

YOUR CURLY BLOND HAIR IS LOVELY...

AND YOUR BLUE EYES ARE QUITE FETCHING.

REALLY! IT LOOKS VERY NICE ON YOU, LIKE A PRETTY FRENCH DOLL.

IT'S ALMOST REHEARSAL TIME. NOW COME ALONG!

NO, NO, IRIS!'

I WANNA STAY AND TALK TO HIM!

AWWW...

WON'T YOU COME TO THE DRESSING ROOM WITH ME?

IRIS, YOU AREN'T GETTING IN OGAMI-SAN'S WAY, ARE YOU?

LET'S GO, IRIS!

HMPH! NEVER MIND.

HUH?

WHAT ARE YOU TALKING ABOUT?

...?? ?

Aaah... Sakura... That hurts!

YOU'RE AWFULLY SMOOTH, AREN'T YOU, OGAMI-SAN?!

....

I GUESS I'VE NEVER HAD MUCH CHANCE TO BE AROUND WOMEN UP TO NOW. THIS JOB IS CERTAINLY FULL OF SURPRISES.

WHO WOULD HAVE THOUGHT THAT SUCH A LITTLE COMPLIMENT WOULD GET SUCH A BIG REACTION?

WHAT IS IT, ENSIGN?

OH, MARIA!

IT'S QUITE STRIKING AGAINST THAT DARK BROWN COSTUME.

I JUST WANTED TO TELL YOU HOW BEAUTIFUL YOUR PLATINUM BLONDE HAIR IS.

WELL, I...

97

OOPS...

I ABHOR SUCH WEAKNESS!

YOU STOPPED ME JUST TO TELL ME THAT?

...SUCH DIFFICULT CREATURES.

WOMEN ARE...

URRRGH...

OF COURSE. TAKE CARE!

I'LL BE BACK LATE, SO KEEP AN EYE ON THIS PLACE WHILE I'M GONE, WILL YOU?

TSUBAKI, I'M GOING OUT ON AN ERRAND OR TWO.

HUT!

AYE, SIR!

HEAD UP! STAND STRAIGHT!

WHAT KIND OF AN ANSWER IS THAT?

YES, SIR...

MASTER NAKAJIMA WILL INSTRUCT YOU ABOUT THE PROPS, ALL RIGHT?

FIX THE PROPS AND DO THE SHOPPING FOR THE KITCHEN BEFORE THE THEATER OPENS, WILL YOU?

OH, AND OGAMI...

GO SAFELY, SIR!

OKAY, I'LL BE BACK.

AND STOP BY THE LIQUOR STORE AND PICK UP SOME SAKE FOR ME.

100

IT'S YOUR TURN TO DO THE NIGHTTIME PATROL, OGAMI-SAN.

I FIGURED YOU'D FORGET.

SAKURA-KUN!

WHAT ARE YOU DOING OUT AT THIS HOUR?

THAT'S RIGHT.

OH...

ARE YOU ALL RIGHT?

UMM...

YOU SEEM A LITTLE DOWN.

OGAMI-SAN...

YOU DON'T HAVE TO COME WITH ME, SAKURA-KUN.

PLEASE, FEEL FREE TO GO TO BED.

YES, BUT...

DON'T WORRY. I CAN DO THE PATROL BY MYSELF...

HA HA HA...

AT NIGHT, THIS IS ONE OF MY FAVORITE PLACES. I LOVE THIS VIEW.

ISN'T IT BEAUTIFUL?

OGAMI-SAN...?

104

...WHAT WILL I BE LEFT WITH?

IF I THROW AWAY THE FACT THAT I'M A SOLDIER...

OGAMI-SAN...

AND ON TOP OF THAT, THE COST IS ASTRONOMICAL.

WELL, IT'S ABSOLUTE LUNACY IN TERMS OF COMMON SENSE.

THERE IS STRONG OPPOSITION IN THE HIGHER RANKS, BUT...

OUR PLAN IS PROCEEDING ON SCHEDULE.

Capital City Defense Plan
Imperial Fighting Troupe
Flower Division Report

I REFUSE TO RELIVE THE TRAGEDIES OF FIVE YEARS AGO.

I UNDERSTAND, COUNT HANAKOJI.

HOWEVER, THE FLORAL ASSAULT SQUAD STRATEGY MUST SUCCEED!

WE FINALLY REBUILT THIS CITY. WE CANNOT LET IT SINK BACK INTO THE ASHES!

OH, HIM.

HEH HEH HEH...

HMM... BY THE WAY, HOW IS HE?

THAT LAD THE NAVY SENT?

...UNLESS MY AGING EYES DECEIVE ME...

HE'S STILL PRETTY GREEN, BUT...

IN ANY CASE, THE FUTURE OF THIS GREAT CITY DEPENDS ON YOU AND YOUR IMPERIAL FIGHTING TROUPE.

I'M COUNTING ON YOU, YONEDA-KUN. YOU'RE OUR ONLY HOPE.

IF YOU SAY SO, HE MUST BE FINE.

I SEE...

The Meaningless Busywork--End of Act

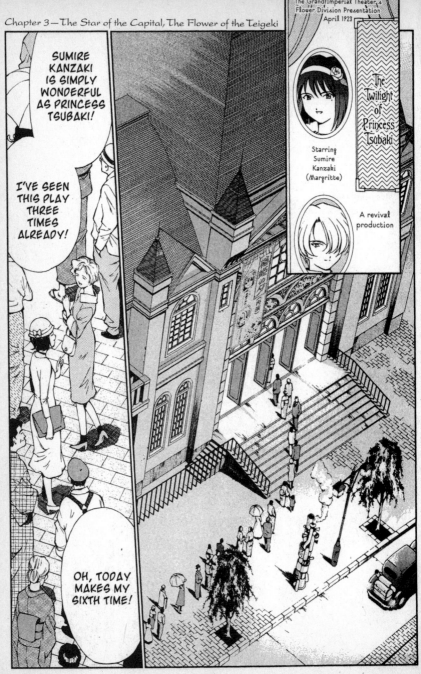

The Grand Imperial Theater's Flower Division Presentation April 1923

The Twilight of Princess Tsubaki

Starring Sumire Kanzaki (Margritte)

A revival production

SUMIRE KANZAKI IS SIMPLY WONDERFUL AS PRINCESS TSUBAKI!

I'VE SEEN THIS PLAY THREE TIMES ALREADY!

OH, TODAY MAKES MY SIXTH TIME!

109

IS THIS WHAT YOU WANT, ICHIRO OGAMI?

EACH DAY I JUST DO WHAT THEY TELL ME TO WITHOUT ANY SENSE OF ACCOMPLISHMENT...

PACHIK

I GUESS IT'S TIME FOR ME TO FACE REALITY.

BUT ALL I EVER DO ARE THESE MENIAL TASKS...

Sigh

THAT'S WHAT IT MEANS FOR A MAN TO WORK.

NO...

EVEN IF IT'S SOMETHING I DON'T CARE ABOUT, I OUGHT TO FIND PURPOSE IN THE JOB I WAS ASSIGNED TO.

UMM...

Please refrain from dancing in the lobby.

. . . . .

HER BEAUTY, HER CLASS AND HER PRESENCE ARE LIKE THOSE OF THE MOST KIND-HEARTED, INNOCENT MAIDEN!

OH, MISS SUMIRE!

SHE IS MY MADONNA!

DON'T YOU AGREE?

HUH?

TELL HER IT'S FROM HER MOST ARDENT FAN!

PARDON ME, BUT COULD YOU PLEASE GIVE THIS TO MISS SUMIRE?

OH, THANK YOU VERY MUCH!

OH, A FAN LETTER.

SURE THING.

SURE...

WELL...

113

114

THE PATRONS ARE COMING TO SEE ME, THE HEROINE OF THIS PLAY.

IT DOESN'T MATTER!

AS LONG AS I CAN SHINE...!

...THE SCRIPT SAYS TO STAND HERE...

B-BUT...

WON'T YOU PLEASE STAND IN A MORE OBSCURE, OUT-OF-THE-WAY LOCATION?

IF YOU STAND THERE, THE AUDIENCE WON'T BE ABLE TO SEE ME.

ARGH!

ぎゅっ

URGH!

LET'S MAKE SOMETHING VERY CLEAR. KINDLY DO NOT GET IN THE WAY OF MY ACTING!

THE FACT THAT I HAVE TO BE ON THE SAME STAGE AS A COUNTRY-BUMPKIN NEWCOMER LIKE YOU IS INSULT ENOUGH!

IF SUMIRE-SAN WERE WEARING A KIMONO, I'D BE STEPPING ON HER HEM...

WELL...

WHAT ON EARTH ARE YOU DOING, SAKURA?

IT'S A SHAME THAT YOU'RE NOT!

"MAR-VELOUS ACTRESS" ...

...YOU SAY?

IS SHE?

I'M BACK!

AAAH. I'M FINALLY HOME.

MAY I HAVE YOUR ATTENTION, PLEASE?

MEETING?

YUP. THE MEETING LASTED FOREVER.

MAN-AGER...

YOU WERE OUT PRETTY LATE, SIR.

WE WILL NOW BEGIN THE PERFORMANCE OF "THE TWILIGHT OF PRINCESS TSUBAKI" BY THE FLOWER TROUPE OF THE IMPERIAL THEATER.

GO AHEAD AND TAKE A BREAK, TOO, OGAMI.

I'LL BE IN MY ROOM RESTING.

EH HEM. NEVER YOU MIND!

SIR.

IT'S NEVER INTERESTED ME, BUT...

DRAMA...

...I GUESS SAKURA-KUN AND IRIS ARE ALSO IN THE PERFORMANCE.

MAYBE I'LL TAKE A PEEK.

......

WOW, IT'S A FULL HOUSE.

THEY'RE ALL SO INTO IT.

SOME ARE EVEN CRYING!

BUT NOW THERE IS NOTHING LEFT FOR ME.

ARMAND'S LOVE WAS THE ONLY THING WORTH LIVING FOR.

OH!

HOW I HAVE CHANGED!

MY ROSY CHEEKS HAVE TAKEN ON THE PALLOR OF DEATH...

SHE ACTUALLY LOOKS AS THOUGH SHE'S QUITE ILL.

SUMIRE-KUN LOOKS DIFFERENT FROM THE WAY SHE LOOKED AT REHEARSAL.

PLEASE FORGIVE ME!

FORGIVE A SINFUL WOMAN WHO LOST HER WAY.

OH LORD...

ALL THE HAPPINESS, THE SADNESS, EVERYTHING.

THIS IS THE END.

SOMETHING INCREDIBLE HAS HAPPENED!

YOU TWO...

WHAT ARE YOU BABBLING ABOUT?

MISTRESS, PLEASE STAY CALM, BUT...

MISTRESS!

MIS-TRESS!

COULD IT BE HIM?

NO, COULD IT BE...?

MARGRITTE!!

AH... IT WAS NOT MEANT TO BE.

MY WISH FINALLY CAME TRUE...

...BUT I CANNOT STAY TO ENJOY IT.

MARGRITTE!!

THAT I AM ABLE TO DIE IN THE ARMS OF MY BELOVED.

IT'S ENOUGH FOR ME...

DON'T LEAVE ME ALONE, MARGRITTE!

YOU MUSTN'T DIE, MY DARLING!

THE LORD CAN'T BE SO CRUEL AS TO LEAD ME HERE ONLY TO FACE SUCH PAIN!

PLEASE HOLD ON, MARGRITTE.

NO! WHAT ARE YOU SAYING?!

YOU MUST LIVE, MARGRITTE!

NO! DON'T DIE!

Sniff...

TAKE THIS PORTRAIT...

THE WOMAN WHO LOVED YOU SO.

...AND THINK OF ME ONCE IN A WHILE.

PLEASE TAKE IT...

...THE IMAGE OF WHAT I ONCE WAS...

...WHO WILL ALWAYS BE WATCHING OVER BOTH OF YOU FROM ABOVE...

...AS A GIFT FROM SOMEONE...

...PLEASE MAKE HER YOUR BRIDE.

AND SHOULD YOU SOME-DAY MEET A LOVELY GIRL WHO IS ENTIRELY DEVOTED TO YOU...

AND GIVE HER THIS...

MIS-TRESS!!

YOUR PERFORMANCE WAS ESPECIALLY GOOD TODAY, SUMIRE.

HMM...I AGREE.

NO MATTER HOW MANY TIMES YOU EXPERIENCE IT, IT'S ALWAYS DELICIOUS, ISN'T IT MARIA-SAN?

THIS SENSE OF RELEASE AFTER A PERFORMANCE...

OH HO HO HO HO...

SPLENDID JOB!

WELL DONE!

I WAS SO SAD, I EVEN CRIED!!

YES! I REALLY FELT AS IF YOU WERE DYING!

SUMIRE-KUN!

SUMIRE-KUN!

AND WHY IS THAT?!

THOUGH IT MIGHT BE A REAL CHALLENGE FOR YOU, SAKURA-SAN...

WELL, YOU TWO--WATCH THE MASTER AND LEARN! PERHAPS YOU MAY EVEN BECOME A GREAT ACTRESS LIKE ME SOMEDAY!

Oh ho ho ho

I WAS WATCHING PRINCESS TSUBAKI, AND I COULDN'T STOP THE TEARS...

BUT THAT PERFORMANCE YOU JUST GAVE...

A MAN SHOULDN'T CRY, BUT I...

TO BE HONEST, I LOOKED DOWN ON WHAT YOU GUYS WERE DOING...

I HAD...

...AS SOME KIND OF FOOLISH CHILD'S PLAY...

...WITHOUT EVER HAVING ACTUALLY WATCHED IT.

I DIDN'T REALIZE DRAMA HAD SUCH POWERS...

AND AT THAT MOMENT...

...AS IF BY SOME KIND OF MIRACLE, I FELT MY WORRIES DISAPPEAR.

UMM...

WELL...

I JUST WANTED TO TELL YOU HOW WONDERFUL THE PERFORMANCE WAS.

I JUST... THAT'S ALL.

ANYWAY...

YOU DO HAVE AN EYE FOR THE REAL THING!

PERHAPS YOU'RE NOT SO BAD, ENSIGN!

IT SEEMS THAT YONEDA-SAN'S SELECTION WAS RIGHT AFTER ALL.

SEE YOU AROUND.

OH HO HO HO HO!

NOT TO MENTION ...

O...OH...

MY APOLO-GIES, MARIA.

PLEASE TAKE YOUR LEAVE NOW.

ENSIGN.

YOUR PRESENCE HERE DISTURBS OUR TEAM-WORK.

· · · · · ·

FORGOT ABOUT THIS FAN LETTER.

OH, SHOOT.

Teigeki's Top Star Miss Sumire Kanzaki

OH, WELL ...

TEIGEKI'S TOP STAR...

133

MORE IMPORTANT THAN BEING MOBSTERS, WE ARE FANS OF THE FLOWER DIVISION!

YOU IDIOT!

AREN'T OUR SAVINGS STARTING TO DWINDLE?

BUT IS IT OKAY TO LEAVE THE BUSINESS ON THE SIDELINES LIKE THIS?

I HAVE NOTHING AGAINST PLAYS, BOSS...

AS FANS, WE MUST SEE EVERY SINGLE PERFORMANCE. THAT'S AN IRON-CLAD RULE!

HEY YOU, LAD.

ENJOY THE SHOW!

WELCOME!

134

NICE SMILE!

WELCOME TO THE IMPERIAL!

WELCOME!

THANKS TO YOU, SIR!

The Star of the Capital, The Flower of the Teigeki-- End of Act

真宮寺さくら　Sakura Shinguji as Ebisu.

Cheep
chireep

chir...

138

GOOD MORNING!

OH, OGAMI-SAN.

YOU'RE UP AND AT 'EM EARLY, SAKURA-KUN.

YOU MUST BE QUITE EXCEPTIONAL.

BUT THERE CAN'T BE THAT MANY ACTRESSES WHO ARE SO ADEPT AT MARTIAL ARTS, CAN THERE?

I STILL HAVE MUCH TO LEARN.

OH, I'M NO EXPERT...

I DIDN'T REALIZE YOU WERE SUCH AN EXPERT.

YOUR SWORDS-MANSHIP IS OUT-STANDING.

IS THAT SO?

I HAD NO IDEA...

MARIA-SAN IS AN EXPERT MARKSMAN, AND SUMIRE-SAN HAS THE TITLE OF FULL MASTERSHIP IN THE NAGINATA IN THE KANZAKI JINRYU STYLE.

NO, NOT AT ALL!

NAGINATA= HALBERD OR LONG SWORD

REIRYOKU= SPIRITUAL/SOUL POWER

142

Asakusa wholesale district

DON'T YOU THINK IT'S STRANGE THAT ALL THE ACTRESSES ARE EXPERTS IN MARTIAL ARTS?

SWORDSMANSHIP, GUNS AND NAGINATA. EVEN REIRYOKU...

BUT WE'RE A THEATRICAL TROUPE!

WHAT IS, OGAMI-SAN?

BUT DON'T YOU THINK IT'S STRANGE?

SO I HAD A VERY EXCITING MORNING.

IT'S ONLY NATURAL THAT THE FLOWER DIVISION IS SO STRONG.

WELL, WELL... THIS IS THE "ERA OF WOMEN" NOW.

I HAVE TO READ THOSE LITERARY MAGAZINES ONCE IN A WHILE.

I'M ONLY A PROP MAN, BUT I STILL AM PART OF THE THEATER TROUPE.

BOY, YOU REALLY KNOW THE CITY.

HE'S PROBABLY HEADED FOR YANAGIBASHI OR SOMETHING.

THAT'S YASUNARI KAWABATA, THE UP-AND-COMING WRITER.

BY THE WAY, THAT YOUNG MAN WHO JUST WENT BY...

WH-WHAT WAS THAT?!

DABOOM!

I ALMOST FORGOT TO BUY 30 FAKE CAMELLIAS.

AH! OOPS!

EVERYBODY AROUND ME SEEMS SO WORLDLY...

ALL CITIZENS EVACUATE IMMEDIATELY!!

EMERGENCY IN THE KURAHASHI AREA!!

I REPEAT-- EMERGENCY IN THE KURAHASHI AREA!!

WAAA

OOOH

clang

clang

clang

LET'S START RUNNING BEFORE WE GET EATEN UP!

YIIEE! SCARY...

OI, OI! YOU DON'T THINK IT'S 'THEM' AGAIN...?

I'M SORRY, BUT YOU GO ON WITHOUT ME!

MASTER NAKA-JIMA...

OGAMI-SAN, WHAT ARE YOU DOING?

WE'VE GOTTA GET OUT FAST!

146

148

151

GET THAT CIVILIAN OUT OF THERE, *NOW!!*

WHAT DO YOU THINK YOU'RE DOING?!

CAPTAIN!

Hff

Haah

ARE YOU HURT?!

HUH?!

HOW DARE YOU CALL YOURSELVES PART OF THE POLICE FORCE?!

YOU SPINELESS IDIOTS!

YOU SHOULD TAKE A CUE FROM THAT...

WE CAN'T FIGHT AGAINST THAT MONSTER!

THAT'S IMPOSSIBLE.

WHAT IS THAT...?!

WHA...

THERE'S NO CHANCE FOR ME TO STRIKE BACK!

IT'S TOO FAST!

UH OH!

159

GRRRRRR EEEEE!!

STAND DOWN! YOU'RE BLOCKING MY ATTACK.

K'ACHUNK

HEY YOU!

THIS WAY. THIS WAY!

Psssssh

A WOMAN IS PILOTING THAT STEAM ROBOT?!

CAN'T BE...

BUT THAT WAS... A WOMAN'S VOICE!

165

166

BUT WHY...?!

THERE'S NO MISTAKING IT.

THAT WAS...

WHO ARE YOU...?

HEY, STOP!

JUST SEND ME BACK TO THE NAVY RIGHT AWAY!

I DON'T CARE!

DON'T YOU LIKE THE IMPERIAL ANYMORE?

YOU WERE COMING ALONG SO WELL!

WHAT ON EARTH IS THE MATTER ALL OF A SUDDEN?

A TERRIFYING MONSTER THAT SPITS FIRE AND FLIES, AND MYSTERIOUS HUMAN-SHAPED STEAM ROBOTS...

BUT AFTER SEEING WHAT I SAW...

IF THE CAPITAL IS SAFE AND PEACEFUL, I WOULD GLADLY TAKE TICKETS AND DO YOUR SILLY CHORES.

AND AS A SOLDIER...NO, AS A *MAN*, I CAN'T JUST SIT BACK AND WATCH IT HAPPEN!!

SOMETHING STRANGE, SOMETHING OUT OF THE ORDINARY AND TERRIBLE IS HAPPENING IN THIS CITY!

THIS IS NO TIME TO BE DRINKING SAKE, SIR!!

HAVE A LITTLE DRINK WITH ME?

NOW, HOW ABOUT WE JUST CALM DOWN A BIT.

SHHH!

SHHH!

GOODNESS, WHAT ARE YOU TWO UP TO?

WHO IS IT?

PLEASE... YOU TWO HAVE SOME OF THE MOST DISTASTEFUL LITTLE HOBBIES. IT'S QUITE SHOCKING!

OH, YOU'RE EAVES-DROPPING.

...WAS PROBABLY A "KOUMA," A FALLEN DEMON.

SOUNDS LIKE THE MONSTER YOU SAW...

HMMM...

THOSE MONSTERS HAVE BEEN APPEARING HERE IN THE CAPITAL TO MAKE TROUBLE SINCE THE BEGINNING OF TIME.

YEP.

A FALLEN DEMON... I KNEW IT.

NOTHING TO BE DONE...

IT WAS ONLY BY THE SKIN OF OUR TEETH THAT WE PREVENTED THE CAPITAL FROM BEING COMPLETELY DESTROYED BACK THEN.

EIGHT YEARS AGO, A LEGION OF FALLEN DEMONS VICIOUSLY ATTACKED THE CAPITAL.

YOU BETTER WATCH IT IF YOU GO FOR A LATE-NIGHT ROMANTIC STROLL.

NOT TO MENTION THAT LATELY MYSTERIOUS STEAM ROBOTS OR, "WAKIJI," HAVE BEEN SPOTTED, TOO.

BUT WEREN'T THE KOUMA ANNIHILATED DURING THE WAR?

YOU'RE TALKING ABOUT THE GREAT DEMON WAR. THAT, AT LEAST, I KNOW ABOUT.

RECENTLY, THEY'VE STARTED TO APPEAR AGAIN FROM TIME TO TIME.

HEH... ABOUT THAT...

HOW CAN YOU SIT THERE SO CALMLY?

THIS COULD BE ONE BIG LEAD-UP TO A SECOND WAR FOR ALL WE KNOW!

...WE'RE ALL IN GRAVE DANGER, AREN'T WE?!

BUT THAT MEANS...

FOR ALL YOUR BRAVE TALK, JUST HOW EXACTLY DO YOU THINK YOU CAN HELP?

PA-THETIC.

IT'S NOT LIKE YOU'RE ANY DIF-FERENT.

WHEN YOU GET TO BE MY AGE, ALL THAT KILLING LOSES ITS APPEAL.

I TOLD YOU A DOZEN TIMES. I'M NOT A FIGHTER ANYMORE.

I TELL YOU, THERE IS NOTHING WE CIVILIANS CAN DO.

I GUESS YOU THINK IT'S FINE TO JUST LEAVE ALL THE DECISIONS TO THE BUREAU-CRATS.

FINE! THEN I'M NOT GOING TO BE ASKING ANYMORE.

I'M **TELLING** YOU THAT I WILL FIND MY OWN WAY TO PROTECT THE CAPITAL!

THAT'S ANCIENT HISTORY.

GOOD DAY!!

YOU ONCE HAD THE REPUTATION OF BEING ONE OF THE BRAVEST GENERALS IN THE ARMY DURING THE RUSSO-JAPANESE WAR.

I'M DISAP-POINTED IN YOU, SIR.

I NEVER THOUGHT I WOULD HEAR SUCH COWARDLY WORDS COME OUT OF YOUR MOUTH!

...THE CAPITAL WOULD BE UTTERLY DESTROYED!

THE FALLEN DEMONS...IF A MONSTER LIKE THE ONE I SAW CAME BACK IN LARGE NUMBERS...

"...JUST HOW EXACTLY DO YOU THINK YOU CAN HELP?"

BLAST!

THAT'S HOW IT SEEMS.

YES...

IS THAT IT?

SO, THE TWO OF THEM TOGETHER STILL COULDN'T COMPLETELY ANNIHILATE IT?

...THAT'S A DIFFICULT PROPOSITION.

OF COURSE, THE BEST THING WOULD BE TO MAKE SOMETHING THAT ALLOWS THE RIDER TO FULLY UTILIZE HER REIRYOKU, BUT...

ALL RIGHT. I'LL TRY MAKING SOME ADJUSTMENTS THEN.

HOWEVER, WE'RE WORKING ON THAT FROM OUR END, TOO.

I WOULD THINK SO.

OH, REALLY?

AH, YES. BY THE WAY, THERE WAS A COMMUNIQUÉ FROM COMMAND.

THEY WANT YOU TO JOIN THEM IN GINZA AS SOON AS YOU'RE DONE HERE.

MUST'VE GOOFED AGAIN.

AW, MAN...

SOME REPORTS SUGGEST THE EXISTENCE OF A LARGER ORGANIZATION ACTING BEHIND THE INCIDENTS.

I'M SURE YOU'RE AWARE OF THE INCREASINGLY FREQUENT APPEARANCES OF THOSE MONSTROUS STEAM MACHINES.

DID SOMETHING BIG HAPPEN?

HOW COME THEY'RE IN SUCH A HURRY?

THIS IS A SITUATION WE DID NOT ANTICIPATE.

APPARENTLY SOMEONE BESIDES THE DEMONS ARE INTERESTED IN THE DOWNFALL OF THE CAPITAL...

YES, SHE HAS ALREADY BEEN ALERTED.

SHE'S PROBABLY ON A SHIP BY NOW.

KANNA-HAN IS COMING BACK SOON, TOO, RIGHT?

TRUTH BE TOLD THOUGH, IT'S KIND OF EXCITING TO HAVE A CHANCE TO SEE EVERY-BODY AGAIN.

ALL RIGHT! I'LL GIVE IT MY ALL.

HMM. SOUNDS PRETTY GRIM.

NOTE: "-HAN" INDICATES THAT SHE HAS A KYOTO ACCENT. IT'S THE EQUIVALENT OF "-SAN."

EH, COME WHAT MAY.

I'D BETTER GET SOME SLEEP WHILE I CAN.

THIS IS SOME STORM BREWING ...

From Sakura to Ogami

Everybody has a period when they are new to things. Reading this manga featuring poor, hapless Ogami (who is drawn so wonderfully with so many different expressions!) and seeing his bewilderment so clearly made me remember the first time I auditioned for anime when I was sixteen. The large empty studio was like the cockpit of a Koubu that made me feel faint from nerves and intensified my sense of being wholly alone. The inorganic microphone was like a Kouma, quietly waiting to attack. I hated it! Everything was so grand and impressive that I felt very small and depressed. The only thing that kept me going was the hope that I would be recognized one day. It was exactly the same as Ogami-san just after he was posted to the Grand Imperial Theater. People must endure many trials, but when they get past them they acquire strength and kindness. As I watch Ogami-san perform and grow, I think of my youth and my strong-headed ways back then, and smile from afar.

**Chisa Yokoyama playing
Sakura Shinguji**

When you peel back the three leaves, you can smell sweet cherry through the slightly wet and translucent thin skin of mochi. It was an elegant, splendid sakura mochi. When I took a bite, the gentle sweetness danced around my mouth, filling me with joy.

In the first flush of spring at the beginning of the 21st Century, two men from Kodansha came with some sakura mochi from Choumei Temple. One was a country-samurai type, Yamamoto, the other the obviously geeky Nomura.

I offered the sweets that they had brought me, excusing myself for my "rudeness" as all Japanese do.

When I reached out for the second mochi, Yamamoto said with a heavy overtone, "Magazine Z would like to do a manga version of Sakura Taisen..."

"Not possible," I said as I grabbed the second mochi.

"Don't say that. Would you please just have a look, please?" Yamamoto spread out a series of penciled pages on the table.

"What the hell's this?" I said.

"He is a new manga artist."

I put the sakura mochi down and looked over the freshly drawn pages.

"Amazing. It looks just like Fujishima-sensei's work."

"You see? You see?" Nomura said gaily as he munched his way through some mochi of his own.

"But you know..."

"No, I understand. I understand your feeling that ___ want it to be Fujishima-sensei's manga, but ___ now, we've gotten an okay from Fujishima- ___ and Sega's already given approval...We ___ Haneda many, many times and begged. ___ ___ing this 'cause I'm drunk or insane. ___ ___kura so much! I want to see more ___ **Sniffle!**" Nomura started his

___ form of Japanese candy, ___ is pounded into a dough ___ ___y filling. Yum!]

Cherry Blossoms Flourish in Otowa

By Ohji Hiroi

Yamamoto began talking slowly as he rubbed Nomura's back as if to soothe him. "All we need is your O.K. for the series to begin. Of course I understand your feeling that *Sakura Taisen* should always be the real thing. That is why Kodansha has pleaded with you many times suggesting different manga writers and editors. And many times we've hit the thick wall created by Fujishima-sensei, Sega and you, causing people to get fired, develop neuroses, defect overseas... Why don't we stop this already? It's not good for you to resist any longer."

The way he put it was interesting. He put on a front of compassion and understanding, but it was really a threat.

I knew. Mr. Kosuke Fujishima is a manga writer of Kodansha's. When we were first planning *Sakura Taisen*, I begged and got to borrow him. Yamamoto was saying that it was time to repay the debt. Country-samurai-type Yamamoto was just as iron-armed as he looked.

"So, it's okay with Fujishima-sensei...?" I asked.
"Yes."
"I'm the only one left..."
"Yes."
"And if I say no?"
"You've worked long enough to know how big this industry is. We are Kodansha, after all."
"Is that a threat?"
"Yes." Yamamoto smiled coldly.

At that moment I remembered that several prominent writers had disappeared after refusing work from Kodansha. I didn't want to end up in the bottom of Tokyo Bay.

"Boy, this manga artist is quite good. His name is Ikku Masa, is it? He's good. But can he handle a whole series?"
"Don't worry about that. We have a Series Reinforcement Isolation Apartment behind Kodansha. We'll have him live there. We'll do our best, 24/7."
" I see."
"So, what do you say?"
"Let's do it. Everyone's been waiting for Sakura's manga." I hated myself at this point.
"Then you'll do the script?"
"What? I have to write it?" In my mind, I was yelling, "You dirty, old con-man, Yamamoto
"Yes, Akahori-san says you ought to." I was completely trapped.
"But I'm kinda busy at the moment." I wanted out somehow.
"Igarashi says hello."

When I heard that name, a cold shiver ran down my spine. Everyone in the industry k
of the "Cold-blooded Igarashi." Women go into labor, politicians bow and Yakuza
shake hands. He is the sharpest of the sharp at Kodansha, the boss of publishing.
"Okay, let's do it! I'll write!"
"Great! Banzai!!"

My mind was a rain storm, threatening to drown my heart. Thus began my tribu
Sakura Taisen's manga.

Ensign Ogami has only just begun his first assignment, and he's already considering handing in his resignation! Punching tickets at the theater doesn't seem to be furthering his goal of defending Tokyo from demonic invaders, but the employees of the Imperial Theater are more than they seem, and Manager Yoneda is no exception. The secret mission of the Flower Troupe is revealed, and Ogami's part in it turns out to be a lot more than he ever could have imagined! However, when the girls suit up for their first major battle against the demon steam suits, they will find that their enemies are quite a bit tougher than expected. Will Ogami's leadership (and budding spiritual powers?!) and the teamwork of the Flower Troupe, honed through many a stage show, be enough to fend off the Kuronosu Council and their demonic hordes?

Find out in Sakura Taisen, Vol. 2!